THE ONE EVENT
AUGUST 2019

BEAUTIFUL PRAYERS
to Inspire Your Soul

Selected & Introduced by
Terry Glaspey

HARVEST HOUSE PUBLISHERS
EUGENE, OREGON

BEAUTIFUL PRAYERS
to Inspire Your Soul

Text copyright © 2016 Terry Glaspey

Published by Harvest House Publishers
Eugene, Oregon 97402
www.harvesthousepublishers.com

ISBN 978-0-7369-6719-8 (hardcover)
978-0-7369-6720-4 (eBook)

Cover and Interior Design by
Dugan Design Group, Bloomington, Minnesota

Scripture quotations are taken from

The Holy Bible, New International Version®, NIV®.
Copyright © 1973, 1978, 1984, 2011 by Biblica, Inc.®
Used by permission. All rights reserved worldwide.

The ESV® Bible (The Holy Bible, English Standard Version®),
copyright © 2001 by Crossway, a publishing ministry of Good News
Publishers. Used by permission. All rights reserved.

The King James Version.

All images in this book were found in the British Library's collections,
are believed to be in the public domain, and can be viewed at www.bl.uk.

Printed in China

16 17 18 19 20 21 22 23 24 /RDS/ 10 9 8 7 6 5 4 3 2 1

To the Reader

IN THE PAGES OF THIS LITTLE BOOK you'll find a collection of some of the world's most beloved prayers—prayers drawn directly from the pages of Scripture, classic prayers from some of the great saints and theologians and writers, and prayers of simple devotion from our own time. These are prayers which are beloved for their beauty of expression, for their soul-searching honesty, for their passionate insight into the depth of God's love and the frailty of our human weakness, and for the clarity with which they say the things that we all sometimes feel, but often don't know how to put into words.

These prayers remind us of the universality of our spiritual longings and experiences. People like Francis of Assisi, Augustine, Martin Luther, and Mother Teresa struggled with many of same temptations as you and me. They also recognized their own inadequacy and were aware of their own sins. At the same time, they knew what it was like to feel almost inexpressible gratitude toward God and were thankful for the motions of grace in their lives. They knew what it was to feel one's heart bursting with praise or to experience the peace that arises from a sense of God's presence. And they knew the embrace of God's love.

When we join with them in prayer, we join a chorus of petitioners whose words echo down through the centuries, many of these prayers having been repeated countless times by people of faith who found focus, solace, and a deeper experience of God through these shared words. Though some Christians might give much greater priority to personal, extemporaneous prayers from the heart, the prayers in this little book show us that written prayers can also be "from the heart," and that their beauty of expression, profound theological insight, and authentic honesty can give us just the words we need to lift our hearts and minds Godward. We have no hesitation about singing hymns of praise that were penned by others, so why should we be shy about using the prayers of others to help us lift our needs and desires to God?

So I invite you to join me in making some of these prayers your own. Pray them slowly, savoring each phrase so that they might become part of your own personal vocabulary of prayer. And return again and again to those which best express your own sentiments or which stir your heart and mind to a new and deeper way of living and believing. May these prayers challenge you, inspire you, comfort you, and draw you closer to God.

Terry Glaspey

God, grant me the serenity to accept
the things I cannot change,
The courage to change the things I can,
And the wisdom to know the difference.

REINHOLD NIEBUHR

L ord, make me an instrument of
    Your peace;
Where there is hatred, let me sow love;
Where there is injury, pardon;
Where there is error, truth;
Where there is doubt, faith;
Where there is despair, hope;
Where there is darkness, light;
And where there is sadness, joy.

O Divine Master, grant that I may
    not so much seek
To be consoled as to console;
To be understood as to understand;
To be loved as to love.
For it is in giving that we receive;
It is in pardoning that we are pardoned;
And it is in dying that we are born to
    eternal life.
Amen.

FRANCIS OF ASSISI

Christ with me, Christ before
me, Christ beside me,
Christ in me, Christ beneath me,
Christ above me, Christ on my right,
Christ on my left, Christ where I lie,
Christ where I sit, Christ where I arise.
Christ in the heart of everyone who
    thinks of me,
Christ in the mouth of everyone who
    speaks to me,
Christ in every eye that sees me,
Christ in every ear that hears me.
Salvation is of the Lord,
Salvation is of the Christ,
May Your salvation, Lord, be ever
    with us.

ST. PATRICK

Prayer is to the spiritual life what
the beating of the pulse and the drawing
of the breath are to the life of the body.

JOHN HENRY NEWMAN

ur Father, which art in heaven,
Hallowed be Thy name.

Thy kingdom come.

Thy will be done in earth,

As it is in heaven.

Give us this day our daily bread,

And forgive us our debts,

As we forgive our debtors.

And lead us not into temptation,

But deliver us from evil:

For Thine is the kingdom, and the

power, and the glory,

Forever. Amen.

THE LORD'S PRAYER
MATTHEW 6:9-13

My Lord God, I have no idea
where I am going.
I do not see the road ahead of me.
I cannot know for certain where it
will lead.
Nor do I really know myself, and the fact
That I think I am following Your will
does not mean
That I am actually doing so.
But I believe that the desire to please You
Does in fact please You.
And I hope I have that desire in all
that I am doing.

I hope that I will never do anything apart
    from that desire.
And I know that if I do this, You will
    lead me by the right road,
Though I may know nothing about it.
Therefore I trust You always, though I
    may seem to be lost
And in the shadow of death.
I will not fear, for You are ever with me,
And You will never leave me to face
    my perils alone.

Thomas Merton

Look upon us, O Lord,
And let all the darkness
    of our souls
    Vanish before the beams
    of Your brightness.
        Fill us with holy love,
And open to us the treasures of
    Your wisdom.
All our desire is known unto You,
Therefore perfect what You
    have begun,
And what Your Spirit has awakened
    us to ask in prayer.
We seek Your face.
Turn Your face unto us and show us
    Your glory.
Then will our longing be satisfied,
And our peace shall be perfect.

St. Augustine

M ost merciful God, we confess
that we have sinned against
Thee in thought, word, and deed;
By what we have done,
And by what we have left undone.
We have not loved Thee with our
    whole heart;
We have not loved our neighbors
    as ourselves.
We are truly sorry and we humbly
    repent.
For the sake of Thy Son, Jesus Christ,
Have mercy on us and forgive us;
That we may delight in Thy will,
And walk in Thy ways,
To the glory of Thy Name.
Amen.

THE BOOK OF COMMON PRAYER

Lord, because You have me,
  I owe You the whole of my love;
  Because You have redeemed me,
I owe You the whole of myself;
Because You have promised so much,
I owe You my whole being.
Moreover, I owe You much more love
  than myself
As You are greater than I,
For whom You gave Yourself,
And to whom You promised Yourself.
I pray You, Lord, make me taste by love

What I taste by knowledge;
Let me know by love
What I know by understanding.
I owe You more than my whole self,
But I have no more,
And by myself I cannot render the whole
   of it to You.
Draw me to You, Lord, in the fullness
   of Your love.
I am wholly Yours by creation;
Make me all Yours, too, in love.

ANSELM

True prayers are like those
carrier pigeons which find their way
so well; they cannot fail to go to
heaven, for it is from heaven
that they came; they are only
going home.

CHARLES SPURGEON

O Heavenly Father, You have
   filled the world with beauty;
Open our eyes to behold Your gracious
   hand in all Your works;
That, rejoicing in Your whole creation,
We may learn to serve You with
   gladness,
For the sake of Him through whom
   all things were made,
Your Son Jesus Christ, our Lord.
Amen.

THE BOOK OF COMMON PRAYER

Lord Jesus Christ, pierce my soul
with Thy love
So that I may always long for
Thee alone,
Who art the bread of angels
And the fulfillment of the soul's deepest desires.
May my heart always hunger and feed upon Thee,
So that my soul may be filled
With the sweetness of Thy presence.
May my soul thirst for Thee,
Who art the source of life, wisdom,
Knowledge, light, and all the riches
Of God our Father.
May I always seek and find Thee,
Think upon Thee,
Speak to Thee
And do all things for
The honor and glory of Thy holy name.
Be always my only hope,
My peace, my refuge
And my help in whom my heart is rooted
So that I may never be separated from Thee.

BONAVENTURE

Lord, make me see
Thy glory in every place.

MICHELANGELO

All things live in You, O God.
You command us to seek You,
And You are always ready to be found.
To know You is life,
To serve You is freedom,
To praise You is joy.
We bless and adore You,
Worship and magnify You,
Thank and love You.

AUGUSTINE

Holy Spirit,
As the sun is full of light, the
ocean full of water, heaven
full of glory,
So may my heart be full of Thee.
Give me Thyself without measure,
As an unimpaired fountain, as
inexhaustible riches.
I bewail my coldness, poverty, emptiness,
imperfect vision,
Languid service, prayerless prayers,
praiseless praises.
Suffer me not to grieve or resist Thee.
Come as power, to expel every rebel lust,
to reign supreme and keep me Thine;
Come as teacher, leading me into all truth,
filling me with all understanding;

Come as love, that I may
	adore the Father, and
	love Him as my all;
Come as joy, to dwell in me,
	move in me, animate me;
Come as light, illuminating the
	Scripture, molding me in its laws;
Come as sanctifier, body, soul, and spirit
	wholly Thine;
Come as helper, with strength to bless and
	keep, directing my every step;
Come as beautifier, bringing order out of
	confusion, loveliness out of chaos.
Magnify to me Thy glory by being
	magnified in me,
And make me redolent of Thy fragrance.

AN ANONYMOUS PURITAN PRAYER

Be joyful in hope, patient in affliction, faithful in prayer.

ROMANS 12:12

O Lord,
Thinking about You,
Being fascinated with
theological ideas and discussions,
Being excited about histories of spirituality
And stimulated by thoughts and ideas
about prayer and meditation,
All of this can be as merely an expression
of greed
As the unruly desire for food, possessions,
or power.
Each day I see again that only You can
teach me to pray,
Only You can let me dwell in Your presence.
No book, no idea, no concept or thing,
will ever bring me close to You,
Unless You Yourself let these instruments
become the way to You.

HENRI J. M. NOUWEN

I have no wit, no words, no tears;
My heart within me like a stone
Is numbed too much for hopes
    or fears.
  Look right, look left, I dwell alone;
I lift mine eyes, but dimmed with grief
No everlasting hills I see;
My life is in the falling leaf:
O Jesus, quicken me.
My life is like a faded leaf,
My harvest dwindled to a husk;
Truly my life is void and brief
And tedious in the barren dusk;
My life is like a frozen thing,
No bud nor greenness can I see:
Yet rise it shall—the sap of Spring,
O Jesus, rise in me.
My life is like a broken bowl,

A broken bowl that cannot hold
One drop of water for my soul
Or cordial in the searching cold;
Cast in the fire the perished thing;
Melt and remold it, till it be
A royal cup for Him my King:
O Jesus, drink of me.

CHRISTINA ROSSETTI

Almighty and eternal God,
So draw our hearts to Thee,
So guide our minds,
So fill our imaginations,
So control our wills,
That we may be wholly Thine,
Utterly dedicated unto Thee;
And then use us, we pray Thee,
As Thou wilt,
And always to the glory and welfare
    of Thy people;
Through our Lord and Savior
    Jesus Christ.
Amen.

THE BOOK OF COMMON PRAYER

I ask You, Lord Jesus,
    To develop in me, Your Lover,
An immeasurable urge towards You,
An affection that is unbounded,
A longing that is unrestrained,
A fervor that throws discretion to
    the winds!
The more worthwhile our love for You,
All the more pressing does it become.
Reason cannot hold it in check,
Fear does not make it tremble,
Wise judgment does not temper it.

RICHARD ROLLE

Prayer is no panacea, no substitute for action. It is, rather, like a beam thrown from a flashlight before us into the darkness. It is in this light that we who grope, stumble, and climb, discover where we stand, what surrounds us, and the course which we should choose. Prayer makes visible the right, and reveals what is hampering and false. In its radiance, we behold the worth of our efforts, the range of our hopes, and the meaning of our deeds.

ABRAHAM HESCHEL

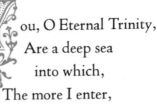

You, O Eternal Trinity,
  Are a deep sea
    into which,
The more I enter,
  the more I find,
And the more I find,
  the more I seek.
O Abyss, O Eternal Godhead,
  O Sea Profound,
What more could You give me
  than Yourself?

Amen.

CATHERINE
OF SIENNA

L ord, end my winter, and let
     my spring begin.
I cannot with all my longing raise my
     soul out of her death and dullness,
But all things are possible with Thee.
I need celestial influences,
The clear shining of Thy love,
The beams of Thy grace,
The light of Thy countenance,
These are the Pleiades to me.
I suffer much from sin and temptation,
These are my wintry signs, my
     terrible Orion.
Lord, work wonders in me, and
     for me.

CHARLES SPURGEON

 God, by whom the meek
are guided in judgment,
And light rises up in darkness
for the godly,
Grant us, in all our doubts and
uncertainties,
The grace to ask what Thou wouldst
have us do,
That the Spirit of wisdom may save
us from all false choices,
And that in Thy light we may
see light,
And in Thy straight path may not
stumble;
Through Jesus Christ our Lord.
Amen.

THE BOOK OF COMMON PRAYER

Prayer is the contact of a
living soul with God. In prayer,
God stoops to kiss man, to bless
man, and to aid in everything
that God can devise or man
can need.

E.M. BOUNDS

Open wide the window of our spirits,
O Lord, and fill us full of light;
Open wide the door of our hearts,
That we may receive and entertain Thee
With all our powers of adoration
and love.

CHRISTINA ROSSETTI

Lord, I know what I ought to ask of You.
You only know what I need.
You know me better than I know myself.
O Father, give to Your child what
he himself
Knows not how to ask.
Teach me to pray.
Pray Yourself in me.

FRANÇOIS FÉNELON

God be in my head,
And in my
understanding;
God be in my eyes,
And in my looking;
God be in my mouth,
And in my speaking;
God be in my heart,
And in my thinking;
God be in my end,
And at my departing.

TRADITIONAL
IRISH PRAYER

Come, Lord, set us on fire.
Clasp us close to Your bosom.
Seduce us with Your beauty.
Enchant us with Your fragrance.
Let us love You.

AUGUSTINE

Teach me, Lord, to sing
of Your mercies.
Turn my soul into a garden,
Where flowers dance in the gentle
breeze,
Praising You with their beauty.
Let my soul be filled with beautiful
virtues;
Let me be inspired by Your Holy Spirit;
Let me praise You always.

TERESA OF AVILA

O Lord, who has mercy upon all,
Take away from me my sins,
And mercifully kindle in me the fire
    of the Holy Spirit.
Take away from me the heart of stone,
And give me a heart of flesh,
A heart to love and
    adore You,
A heart to delight in You,
To follow and to enjoy You,
For Christ's sake.

AMBROSE OF MILAN

Thou hast given so much to me
Give me one thing more—a grateful heart:
Not thankful when it pleaseth me,
As if Thy blessings had spare days,
But such a heart whose pulse may be
Thy praise.

GEORGE HERBERT

Prayer is keeping
company with God.

CLEMENT OF
ALEXANDRIA

Alone with none but Thee, my God,
I journey on my way.
What need I fear, when Thou
     art near,
O King of night and day?
More safe am I within Thy hand
Than if a host did round me stand.

COLUMBA

Teach us, good Lord, to serve You
     as You deserve:
To give and not count the cost;
To fight and not heed the wounds;
To toil and not seek for rest;
To labor and not ask for reward;
Save that of knowing that we
     do Your will.

IGNATIUS OF LOYOLA

You will call on
me and come and pray to
me, and I will listen to you.

JEREMIAH 29:12

Lord, You have
given us Your Word
For a light to shine upon
our path;
Grant us so to meditate
on that Word,
And to follow its teaching,
That we may find in it the
light that shines
More and more until the
perfect day;
Through Jesus Christ,
our Lord.

JEROME

We bless You, O most high God
and Lord of mercy,
You are ever doing numberless great and
inscrutable things with us,
Glorious and wonderful;
You grant to us sleep for rest from our
infirmities
And repose from the burdens of our
much-toiling flesh.
We thank You that You have not destroyed
us in our sins,
But have loved us as ever.
And though we are sunk in despair,
You have raised us up to glorify Your power.
Therefore we implore Your incomparable
goodness,

Enlighten the eyes of our understanding
And raise up our mind from the heavy
    sleep of indolence;
Open our mouth and fill it with Your
    praise,
That we may be able undistracted to
    sing and confess You,
God glorified in all and by all,
The eternal Father,
With Your only-begotten Son,
And Your holy and good and life-giving
    Spirit,
Now and ever, and the ages of ages.
Amen.

BASIL THE GREAT

48

 LORD, in the morning you
hear my voice;
In the morning I prepare a sacrifice
for you and watch.
For you are not a God who delights
in wickedness;
Evil may not dwell with you.
The boastful shall not stand before
your eyes…
I, through the abundance of your
steadfast love,
Will enter your house.
I will bow down toward your holy
temple
In the fear of you.
Lead me, O LORD, in your righteousness
Because of my enemies;
Make your way straight before me.

PSALM 5:3-8

Almighty God, who created us
in Your image:
Grant us grace fearlessly to contend
against evil
And to make no peace with oppression;
And that we may reverently use
our freedom,
Help us to employ it in the
maintenance of justice
In our communities and among
the nations,
To the glory of Your holy Name;
Through Jesus Christ our Lord,
Who lives and reigns with You and the
Holy Spirit,
One God, now and for ever.
Amen.

THE BOOK OF COMMON PRAYER

My God, I love Thee above all else
And Thee I desire as my last end.
Always and in all things, and with
my whole heart, and strength
I seek Thee.
If Thou give not Thyself to me,
Thou givest nothing;
If I find Thee not,
I find nothing.
Grant to me, therefore, Most loving God,

That I may ever love Thee for Thyself
    above all things,
And seek Thee in all things in this
    life present,
So that at last I may find Thee
And keep Thee forever in the world
    to come.

THOMAS BRADWARDINE

O God, early in the morning
I cry to You.
Help me to pray and to concentrate
my thoughts on You;
I cannot do this alone.

DIETRICH BONHOEFFER

Thank You, Lord Jesus,
That You will be our hiding place
Whatever happens.

CORRIE TEN BOOM

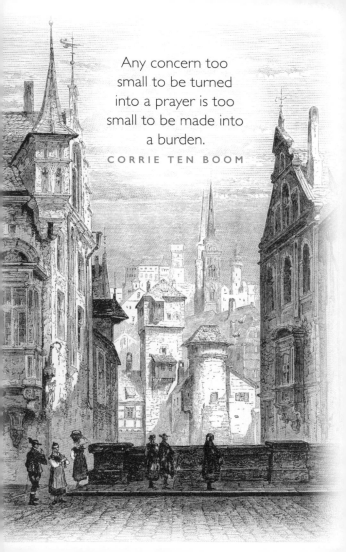

Any concern too small to be turned into a prayer is too small to be made into a burden.

CORRIE TEN BOOM

Use me, then, my Savior,
For whatever purpose, and
in whatever way
Thou may require.
Here is my poor heart,
An empty vessel;
Fill it with Thy grace.
Here is my sinful and
troubled soul;
Quicken it and refresh it with Thy love.
Take my heart for Thine abode;

My mouth to spread abroad

The glory of Thy name;

My love and all my strength,

For the advancement of Thy gospel;

And never suffer the steadfastness

And confidence of my soul to abate;

So that at all times I may be

Enabled from the heart to say,

"Jesus needs me, and I am His."

DWIGHT L. MOODY

Everyone who asks receives; the one who seeks finds; and to the one who knocks, the door will be opened.

MATTHEW 7:8

ather, forgive the cold
love of the years,
While here in the silence we bow,
Perish our cowardice! Perish our fears!
Kindle us, kindle us now.

Lord, we believe, we accept, we adore,
Less than the least though we be.
Fire of love, burn in us, burn evermore
Till we burn out for Thee.

AMY CARMICHAEL

God of love, whose
compassion never fails;
We bring before You
The troubles and perils of
people and nations,
The sighing of prisoners and captives,
The sorrows of the bereaved,
The necessities of strangers,
The helplessness of the weak,
The despondency of the weary,
The failing powers of the aged.
O Lord, draw near to each;
For the sake of Jesus Christ our Lord.

ANSELM

Be, Lord,
Within me to strengthen me,
Without me to preserve,
Over me to shelter,
Beneath to support,
Before me to direct,
Behind me to bring back,
Round about me to fortify.

LANCELOT ANDREWES

I believe; help my unbelief!

MARK 9:24

Here, Lord, is my life.
I place it on the altar today.
Use it as You will.

ALBERT SCHWEITZER

Grant, O God,
That amidst all the
discouragements,
Difficulties and dangers,
Distress and darkness of this
mortal life,
I may depend upon Thy mercy,
And on this build my hopes,
As on a sure foundation.
Let Thine infinite mercy in
Jesus Christ
Deliver me from despair,
Both now and at the hour of death.

THOMAS WILSON

To pray is to dream in
league with God, to envision
His holy visions.
ABRAHAM HESCHEL

From the cowardice that
shrinks from new truths,
From the laziness that is content
with half-truths,
From the arrogance that thinks
it knows all truth.
O God of truth, deliver us.

AUTHOR UNKNOWN

Lord, help me not to despise
or oppose
What I do not understand.

WILLIAM PENN

O God, in whom nothing can live
    But as it lives in love,
Grant us the spirit of love
Which does not want to be
Rewarded, honored, or esteemed,
But only to become the blessing
And happiness of everything
    that wants it;
Love which is the very joy of life,
And thine own goodness and truth
    within the soul;
Who Thyself art Love, and by love
    our Redeemer,
From eternity to eternity.

WILLIAM LAW

orgive me, Lord, my sins—
The sins of my youth, the sins
of the present;
The sins I laid upon myself in an ill
pleasure,
The sins I cast upon others in an
ill example;
The sins that are manifest to all the world,
The sins which I have labored to hide
From mine acquaintance,
From mine own conscience,
And even from my memory;
My crying sins and my whispering sins,
My ignorant sins and my willful;
Sins against my superiors, equals,
servants,
Against my lovers and benefactors,

Sins against myself, mine own body,

Mine own soul,

Sins against Thee, O Almighty Father,

O Merciful Son, O blessed Spirit of God.

Forgive me, O Lord, through the merits
    of Thine anointed,

My Savior, Jesus Christ.

JOHN DONNE

Behold, Lord,
An empty vessel that
needs to be filled.
My Lord, fill it.
I am weak in the faith,
Strengthen me.
I am cold in love;
Warm me and make me fervent
That my love may go out to
my neighbor.
I do not have a strong and firm faith;
At times I doubt and am unable to
trust You altogether.
O Lord, help me.
Strengthen my faith and trust
in You.

MARTIN LUTHER

You are holy, Lord, the only God and
Your deeds are wonderful.
You are strong, You are great,
You are the most high, You are almighty.
You, Holy Father, are King of heaven
and earth.
You are Three and One, Lord God,
all good.
You are good, all good, supreme good,
Lord God, living and true.

You are love, You are wisdom.

You are humility, You are endurance.

You are rest, You are peace.

You are joy and gladness, You are justice
and moderation.

You are all our riches,
and You suffice for us.

You are beauty, You are gentleness.

You are our protector, You are our
guardian and defender.

You are courage, You are our haven
and hope.

You are our faith, our great consolation.

You are our eternal life, great and
wonderful Lord.

God almighty, merciful Savior.

FRANCIS OF ASSISI

most merciful Redeemer,
friend, and brother;
May we know You more clearly,
Love You more dearly,
And follow You more nearly,
Day by day.
Amen.

RICHARD OF CHICHESTER

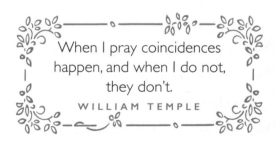

When I pray coincidences
happen, and when I do not,
they don't.

WILLIAM TEMPLE

O Lord, my heart is all a prayer,
  But it is silent unto Thee;
I am too tired to look for words,
I rest upon Thy sympathy
To understand when I am dumb,
And well I know Thou hearest me.

AMY CARMICHAEL

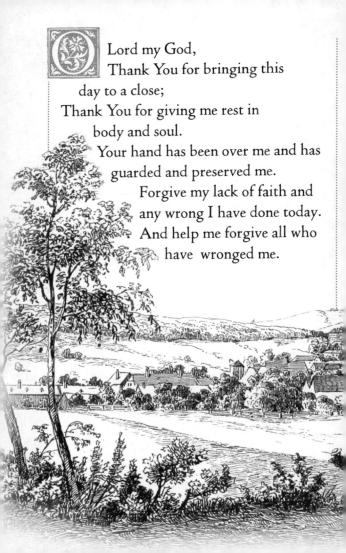

O Lord my God,
    Thank You for bringing this
  day to a close;
Thank You for giving me rest in
    body and soul.
      Your hand has been over me and has
      guarded and preserved me.
        Forgive my lack of faith and
        any wrong I have done today.
        And help me forgive all who
          have wronged me.

Let me sleep in peace under Your
    protection,
And keep me from the temptations
    of darkness.
Into Your hands I commend my loved
    ones and all who dwell in this house;
I commend to You my body and soul.
O God, Your holy name be praised.
Amen.

DIETRICH BONHOEFFER

The LORD is near to all who call on
him, to all who call on him in truth.

PSALM 145:18

*You
Might Also
Enjoy...*

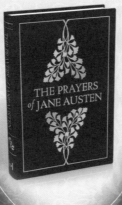